OFF THE GRID

WHY I CAN'T HEAR FROM GOD

ERIC G. ZEIDLER

The Glory Cloud Publications

Copyright © 2016 by Eric G. Zeidler.

All rights reserved. No part of this publication may be reproduced, distributed or transmitted in any form or by any means, including photocopying, recording, or other electronic or mechanical methods, without the prior written permission of the publisher, except in the case of brief quotations embodied in critical reviews and certain other noncommercial uses permitted by copyright law. For permission requests, write to the publisher, addressed "Attention: Permissions Coordinator," at the address below.

Copyright © 2016 by Eric G. Zeidler
Published by: The Glory Cloud publications LLC
PO Box 193, Sicklerville NJ 08081
Theglorycloudpublications.com
Cover Design & Typesetting—TGC publications
Cover Photography — Public Domain
Printed by Ingram Sparks
Book Layout ©2016 BookDesignTemplates.com & TGC publications

Ordering Information: Contact Eric G. Zeidler----- or
The Glory Cloud publications LLC PO Box 193 Sicklerville NJ 08081

Off The Grid/ Eric G. Zeidler —1st ed.
ISBN 978-0-9889866-6-4

Dedication

This book is dedicated to all the pastors, leaders, and those who over the years have tried to enforce to their congregations, and those they disciple, to get OFF THE GRID and seek the Lord.

I want to thank my immediate family Alan, Roland, Chocky (my mom), and Paul (my father). I thank my daughters—Deziree, Richelle, along with the many friends I grew up with in Penns grove in my early years. Much thanksgiving I offer to my wife Jaimie for over 35 years of marriage and learning the peace and joy we have in Him.

Additionally, I thank MaryAnn and Kevin Jordan for allowing me to complete this book in a peaceful place. Likewise, thanks to Kristi Nestel for photographic artistry capturing me OFF THE GRID. And, a special thanks to Minister Terrence Clark for encouraging me, and working with me, on this project.

Foremost, thanking the most important person—Jesus Christ—my Lord and Savior for walking with me, and showing me that He will never leave me. In due honor, I thank God—the Holy Spirit for guiding me in this book and God—my Father for allowing me the experiences to write this book whereby encouraging others to seek Him.

"Every new day begins with possibilities. It's up to us to fill it with the things that move us toward progress and peace."

—Ronald Reagan

Contents

The Way We Used To Be 1

Emotions 13

What Is Off The Grid? 25

Being the Voice 37

The Presence Of The Lord 49

Why We Need To Get Off The Grid 59

Conclusion 67

Workbook 73

Chapter One
The Way We Used To Be

Looking back on all the many years that have gone by, the way serving Christ has changed over the past fifty-nine years of my life, I have to stop and ponder. I reflect on, what has caused us as Christians to be a people who love the Lord, attend church, and still feel empty at times?

This book is written to share those experiences of when I first heard the Lord's voice. I recall, when I first felt HIM everywhere I went. I remember, the time when I first cried because I could feel HIS presence. I remember those times, clearer as the Lord began to reveal the days of my past to me. I share these, my experiences with the hopes that all Christian believers, in these last days, would rekindle as a body, the hunger, passion, presence, and heart of HIM who died for us—JESUS, that name above every name.

This book shares the testimonies, as examples, of how God can take someone who is open and willing to be stretched, and use them for HIS

Glory and HIS purpose. This book, I believe, is a wake-up call to believers who have lost or who have become immersed in the world for far too long.

> John 17:15, 16—I pray not that thou shouldest take them out of the world, but that thou shouldest keep them from the evil. They are not of this world, even as I am not of the world.

The message in this book, I pray, will help you get back to your daily walk with JESUS and the HOLY SPIRIT. A journey that will lead you and guide you in righteousness, peace, and joy.

In this chapter, I will share with you the way things used to be. The way families, like mine, grew up going to church. The way we as a family would go about our daily lives. For some, this will bring back memories—some good and some not so good. The goal is to remember what it was like to chill, enjoy being with family and friends. Most of all, its remembering the holy presence of God and the blessings experienced during those times. Stop, in this moment, and think about how far apart we have drifted in our relationship to Christ. How we have come to a place it seems, that we can't hear from God as we used to.

It's Sunday morning and you pull the covers up over your head pretending to be sleeping. Consciously knowing you had to go to church, hoping maybe, just maybe, mom and dad would say, "Go ahead, sleep in this morning." At the time, you did not understand that mom and dad were using a very important blessing scripture.

> Proverbs 22:6—Train up a child in the way he should go, and when he is old, he will not depart from it.

Preparing for church meant—putting on your Sunday best, dressing not to impress anyone (but because it was the way it was), stuffing feet into *Hush Puppies*, as it was with me. Shoes still not broken in, because they were only worn for good or special events. CHURCH, was a big event.

The norm was riding in the car as a family (not separate cars). We'd be all dressed up and made to go, all because it's Sunday. Everyone goes to church on Sunday. We rode pass empty stores—closed, because it's Sunday. All stores are closed on Sunday. Why? Because, it's Sunday.

We walk into church, for Sunday School. There were no games, food or snacks, or anything that would entice kids to go. You were there because you learned about Jesus and the Bible on Sunday. I remember learning scripture, Old and New Testament stories of the Bible. We learned—sitting still, quiet, and behaved. Why?—because, it's Sunday. It's Sunday School and that's how we behaved at church.

After Sunday School we went to the sanctuary for the service. The sanctuary was a holy and reverent place. It was a place that you respected. It was a place where as a child, teen or adult, we were quiet, still, and no clowning around. Although we didn't want to be there, we had to, because on Sunday, church is what you do. There was not a social time where coffee was served or snacks, like donuts, were available. There was no time for catching up on lost conversation with others we haven't seen in a week—sharing about the football picks, or what team is playing that Sunday.

We sat and listened to the pastor share the scriptures, repeating the creed—we all believed in, and yes, taking communion once a month. During the service, we would sing the old hymns with excitement.

There was only an organ that played. No drums, no guitars, and no bass. There was a choir that sang along with the congregation and there seemed to be a joyful, yet somber attitude throughout the service.

After church, it was family time—lunch together, maybe a ride somewhere in the afternoon (as a family), home around four o'clock, with just enough time for mom to make dinner. We sat down together (as a family) eating while talking about things that were going on in each other's life. We reviewed the week, in school, in sports, or at dad's workplace. The conversation never went to other people, things in the news, or current events. The topic of conversation was always about us as a family. When dinner was finished, we all had about an hour to do something we liked to do. Mine was taking the comics from the Sunday paper, sketching or re-drawing the cartoons on another piece of paper. I loved waiting until after church, stopping by the paper store in *Penns Grove*, and getting the Bulletin, to see what was new in the comic pages.

Then came the highlight of the week and Sunday—*The Wonderful World of Disney*. Yep, it was family time in front of the black and white TV. Alan, Roland and myself would sit on the floor, while mom and dad would sit on the couch. Every week, we would repeat the same thing. It was a constant. It was comfortable. It was Sunday. The best day of the week. To end a beautiful day, it was time for prayers and bed. No telephone, no Internet, no Game-boy, no *X-box*, and no interruptions. It was just *Off the Grid* time—just peace, rest, and family time. That was the way it used to be.

With time, comes change. Like most growing up, I started to look at things in a different light. As I shifted into high school, I thought I knew what was best for me---WHAT A JOKE! On Sundays, I still went to Church and to Sunday School. Except now, it is called "youth group." It was where teens gathered and talked about things currently happening in school, or should I say, talk about people in school. Growing up, youth lose focus on what is really important. Many, never gain that knowledge as an older saint. What is lost, it seems, is the desire, the reverence, and even the quiet times—to just sit, and be still, and let God be God.

ON THE GRID is a term that I will be using throughout this book to show the difference of being "caught up in the world" or "being in the flesh." Accordingly, verses and references to "walking in the spirit" or "being in His presence" will be termed *Off the Grid*.

> Romans 8:12-14—Therefore, brethren, we are debtors, not to the flesh, to live after the flesh. For if we live after the flesh, ye shall die, but if ye through the Spirit do mortify the deeds of the body, ye shall live. For as many as are led by the Spirit of God, they are the sons of God.

Teenagers are very impressionable beings. Desiring to be on their own, yet deep down inside, realizing that their parents, teachers, and those in authority are [I guess] right. For a teen, without the grounding of the Word of God (and sometimes with it) in their life, could lead to stepping out into the world of lust, drugs, alcohol, and sex. Unbeknownst, that behind that world, what awaits, is a fall, and some will fall hard. As a teenager, I did a lot of stuff that was not right or honorable in the sight of God. Again, as in *Proverbs 22:6—Train up!* I am so thankful for my mom and dad, for waking me up, when I was tired, having me put on my Sunday best, dragging me to church and Sunday School to learn about Jesus, the Word of God through stories, and sermons that were preached in church. Although then I did not understand, but I listened, and received the Word to grow.

You see, today, I have learned that being ON THE GRID or being OFF THE GRID is a choice we must decide each and every day. It's a choice that will either blind us from spiritual things or heighten our senses to the moving of God. A choice to walk in the Spirit of God or to walk in the flesh—the worldly way, which is the way of destruction. How we grow up forms the image or mold by which we live out our lives. We can be formed, like a mold, in a certain way, yet change, by allowing things to transform us through trials, which is character building.

Years ago, a friend of mine, *Peg*, who has gone to be with the Lord, taught me a very valuable lesson. It was one day, while I was watching her mold and form a pot on the potter's wheel. What God showed Jeremiah, he showed me that day.

> Jeremiah 18: 1-6—The word which came to Jeremiah from the Lord, saying, Arise, and go down to the potter's house, and there I will cause thee to hear my words. Then I went down to the potter's house, and, behold, he wrought a work on the wheels. And the vessel that he made of clay was marred in the hand of the potter's; so he made it again another vessel, as seemed good to the potter to make it. Then the word of the Lord came to me, saying, O house of Israel, cannot I do with you as the potter? saith the Lord. Behold, as the clay is in the potter's hand, so are ye in mine hand, O house of Israel.

This scripture became so real to me that day. Peggy was sitting outside in front of the potter's wheel. I was walking by and became very curious to what she was doing. She called me over and started to share with me the Jeremiah scripture showing me as she was forming a piece of clay. She started by saying, "This is an example of what God will do in our lives *if only* we would allow Him to form exactly what He wants in us." Grabbing a lump of clay, Peggy said, "You just can't throw a piece of clay right on the wheel and start turning it. It is too hard, and too stiff. You have to first start stretching the clay, forcing pressure on it, then stretching it some more, just like making flour and water for dough." I was looking at this frail body in a wheel chair, a woman barely one hundred and ten pounds, handle this clay into shape.

I was thinking, "wow, it doesn't take massive muscles, just pressure, and consistency."

Peggy said, "The more you apply pressure and knead it, the easier it is to work when you put it on the wheel."

Wow, isn't that like first coming to the Lord? He stretches us, and prepares us for the wheel of spiritual growth. After about fifteen to twenty minutes of kneading and stretching, the clay is ready. Peggy said, "You take the clay and place it in the *center* of the wheel. You must place it there, or the clay will start to wobble and collapse." Again, thinking about how without Jesus in the center of our lives (or our focus), we start to wobble out of sync, and fall over (or crash). Then Peggy shared the most valuable lesson as she explained, "Now once the clay is in the center, you can start the wheel. But, you now have to apply water on a regular basis to do anything." Think about this, The Word of God is the water applied to our lives that makes it easy to digest and understand the way we need to live our lives. The more water (God's Word) we apply to our lives, the easier it is to live a life full of grace, joy, love and peace.

As Peggy continued explaining the process, I had one of those God-Holy Spirit moments. A "kairos" moment, a moment when God speaks to you in a special way. As Jeremiah went to the potter's house, I too, am now sitting in front of the potter's wheel hearing what he heard from the Lord. "Cannot I do with you as the potter?" Then it all started to make sense. God was teaching me at that time how to walk in His presence, walk in the Spirit, learning to be "Off the Grid".

Now Peggy has my attention! She continues to apply the water (Word) with her hands, forming it, applying more water, pushing and pulling the clay into what she had on her mind to make. The clay was pliable, it was not resisting, but moving along with her hands. The perfect position to be with God.

As Peggy finished, she shared with me another valuable lesson from the potter's wheel and the clay. Once she removed the clay it had to be fired. Being "fired" is going into a kiln or furnace to harden and finished it. Peggy placed the clay into the kiln and turned the temperature up to a very high heat. I noticed there was no timer? I asked her, "How do you know when the clay is done?"

Peggy looked at me with the eyes of Christ, and said, "When you take the clay out and pluck it with your finger, if it makes a 'daaa' sound or a dead sound, the clay needs to go back into the fire for it is not ready yet. It's when you pull it out and you pluck it, it rings or sings, it is ready to be brought out and decorated."

Singing, praising, that's the key. When we are ON THE GRID, we sing praises to ourselves, we take the credit. But when we give God the glory, give Him the praise, we are ready to be promoted and decorated to show Him off. When Peggy gave me that very valuable life lesson it changed my life forever, I have learned throughout the years to give God the praise in good times and in bad. When we as Christians are ON THE GRID, we think of one thing—Me. When we are OFF THE GRID, we are in a place of humility, joy, and servant hood.

Here's another life lesson you may be able to relate too. Growing up with two older brothers (Alan and Roland), was an experience that only the youngest in the family could appreciate. It meant hand me downs—clothing (that was not my style), pants (that didn't fit), bikes, toys, sporting goods, and everything else. My experiences as a child growing up with hand me downs never really bothered me. The thing that stayed with me however, was the expectations from my dad that continued, especially in the first few years of ministry.

My father, Paul, was a faithful, loving, man who always provided and *always* knew how to talk to people. I guess that's where I get it from. My dad was the best at planning vacations, although as a young boy it didn't seem that way. We would always go on vacation the third week of August, which was my birthday week. How many kids do you know that go away on their birthday week each year? Amusingly, it wasn't to celebrate my birthday, it was my dad's vacation week. I always said it was my week (laughing).

What do I mean by my dad's expectations? My two older brothers and I were very sports minded and active. My dad's attitude was that we could always do better, no matter how good we thought we were. Can you imagine, never really meeting the goal, or getting the prize? In every aspect of our lives, we were always encouraged to do better. Whether in sports, school, *Boy Scouts*, the YMCA, reading, etc. I think you get it. Every aspect of our lives was trying to obtain something we could never obtain.

I remember one day that crushed my dream. I played little league baseball from an early age. Almost every boy in *Penns Grove* and *Carney's Point* played baseball. It was the thing to do, like going to church on Sunday was the thing to do. There were three little league fields we played on. *Field Number One* was the main field that had large stands. The food concession stand was there also, and when you played on that field, it seemed like you were playing at *Connie Mack* stadium in *Philadelphia*. This one game my dad was standing over by the gate next to the dugout watching his youngest play—me. When I was on the field,

I would glance over to the side fence, where my dad was standing, looking for approval from him. This one particular inning, I was up to bat. I remember it just like it was yesterday,

The first pitch I let go, you always let the first pitch go as a batter, or at least that is what the coach always told us to do. The next pitch came in and it looked like it was in slow motion, like you see on TV. It was a perfect pitch to hit, a long fly ball. I stepped forward, swung the bat, followed through, and all I heard was *Crack!* The ball took off over center field. Back, back, back, and as *Harry Kalous* would say, "IT'S OUTTA HERE!" Yes, a home run, or a homer as we would say. I started running the bases like *Babe Ruth*, *Ty Cobb*, and *Frankie Robison*, touching every base, with a smile that you could not rub off. Rounding third, the team came out to home plate to greet me. What an experience for a young boy. As I touched home plate, my team mates, rubbed my head, patted my back, and said "Great job." Now I needed to hear that from my dad, that great news of joy. I walked over to the fence, my dad standing there with a smile, looking all proud, before saying to me, "Rick, awesome hit, but you know you can hit the ball further." My heart sank. I thought maybe, just maybe, I could have reached that mark, that goal, that place of acceptance.

It wasn't until years later after I was married to Jaimie and owned a screen printing shop in Swedesboro, NJ. The shop was called, *Creative Arts Studio*, and when we started it, it was just Jaimie and I working together to accomplish the American Dream. I remember after the first week we opened, after pouring money, sweat and time into opening up the shop that I had a surprise that shocked me.—My dad!

The door opened and in walked my father, unexpectedly, and holding a bouquet of flowers. At first I thought, it's not Jaimie's birthday? Why would dad bring flowers? He walked up to me, handed them to me and said, "Rick, I am very proud of you." I lost it. The words I wanted to hear all my life. The words that changed my whole day and my life until now. Yes, you got it, I am in tears right now as I am writing this for you. It doesn't end here.

Well, later on in my life, I realized that my dad was classified as a "negative enforcement" teacher. Someone who means well, but encourages someone with a different means of doing so. Believe you me, I look back and thank God for him. I am grateful, even in those days that I did not understand, those lessons made me excel harder and harder.

Now, God has put me into full time ministry, and I still have that desire to be accepted, recognized, and a little pat on the back once in a while. In ministry, we need to be very careful. This is what I mean. The more it seemed that God was opening doors, the more I would say yes. I wanted nothing more but to please God in every aspect of the ministry I was doing. Whether handing out food, ministering to children, handing out tracks, or sharing the good news one on one, the goal was the same—to please God. For about two years, I was going, and going, and going, just like to bunny full of energy. One night, while I was praying, I asked God, "Why does it feel like I am doing so much, yet accomplishing very little, and it seems no one appreciates it?"

It was right there, in that question. I was looking for someone to pat me on the back. I was looking for appreciation and acknowledgment. Listening closely, there was a *spirit of pride* speaking also. Inside me, I heard that small still voice. "Are you really doing it for me, or to please someone? Maybe you were trying to please your dad. I accept you just the way you are. When I ask you to do something, and you do it, I will acknowledge you. I will say good job son."

Wow, what a difference that moment made in my life. It was no longer having to worry about pleasing someone, or others, but just pleasing Him.

So what does God want? He must want me to do works. It is works to achieve recognition, works to achieve glory and fame—Right? No! God loves us no matter how good we are. In our own human efforts, the question is how good is good? What if we have to be ninety-percent good to get to heaven, and miss it by being eighty-nine percent good? How do I gauge what classifies the scale of being good?

> Matthew 19:16,17—And behold, one came and said unto him, Good Master, what good thing shall I do, that I may have eternal life? And he said unto him, Why callest thou me good? There is none good but one, that is God, but if thou wilt enter into life, keep my commandments.

> Ephesians 2:8, 9—For by grace are ye saved through faith, and that not of yourselves, it is a gift of God: Not of works lest any man should boast.

So, there is no scale. There is no means of measure.

Being *Off the Grid*, helps us to get out of the field of play where we strive to achieve greatness, fame, or recognition of our own desire. Being *Off the Grid* releases us from needing to feel accepted by someone, or needing that oozy good feeling when someone looks at us and says great job. It's the place where we're able to walk in joy and in peace, knowing that it doesn't matter how far we hit the ball, or whether it is a home run or not? It's just desiring to please an awesome God that already thinks we are pretty awesome just the way we are. Being *Off the Grid* is just the start of learning to walk with Him, learning to trust in Him alone, and learning to walk in that peace and joy. "Get the message, stop striving and start living!"

Chapter Two
Emotions

One factor that can keep us from experiencing the presence of God is our emotions.

> 1 Corinthians 2:14—But the natural man receiveth not the things of the Spirit of God for they are foolishness unto him; neither can he know them, because they are spiritually discerned.

> Genesis 2:7—And the LORD God formed man of the dust of the ground, and breathed into his nostrils the breath of life; and man became a living soul.

As "human beings", we live in two worlds or two kingdoms. Human consciousness in this earth is alive through the use of five senses that God has given to us. By them, we perceive the biological world. These senses are to operate in this world and this world only. He has given us:

Sight—the ability to see His beauty, and the things around us. We can be deceived by what we see in the natural man's kingdom.

2 Corinthians 5:7—For we walk by faith, not by sight.

With our eyes, we cannot walk in God's kingdom by what we see in the natural world. Our physical sight is for the purpose of only visually perceiving and gauging what is around us in the physical realm.

Hearing—the ability to hear, listen and communicate from one person to another, in the flesh, here on this physical realm only. It is also used to warn us of danger, or things behind or above us. It is used for the purpose of gathering, retaining, and using information.

James 1:22—But be ye doers of the word, and not hearers only deceiving your own selves.

Touch—the ability to physically feel something, or touch with the fingers. The purpose is to feel sensations such as heat, cold, pointy, or round. This is only used in the physical realm to touch and register in our mind that which we feel.

Hebrews 4:15—For we have not a high priest which cannot be touched with the feeling of our infirmities; but was in all points tempted like as we are, yet without sin.

Taste—the ability to eat, and experience variables like hot and cold, spicy and sweet, sour and spoiled. Taste is used to bring an awareness to the brain the type of substance we are putting into our mouth. This is only used for items that grow or are made from on this earth.

Matthew 15:11—Not that which goeth into the mouth defileth a man; but that which cometh out of the mouth, this defileth a man.

Smell—the ability to take particles from the air that enters the nostrils and discern from what the aroma came. It registers to the brain feelings of enjoyment or distaste—bitter or foul. Its purpose is also to prompt the brain to use all the senses bringing a type of pleasure or emotion.

These senses again, are for the purpose of using them while we are here on this earth. However, we can mix up these senses by trusting in them, which can cause us to operate ON THE GRID, which takes us away from the very presence of God.

Now, there is another factor involved with our emotions. God has produced in our lives the ability to enjoy and have pleasure while here on this earth. This is where we get into trouble. God's plan for us was to seek Him first, not ourselves. This is the *Endorphins* factor.

Endorphins are the body's natural opiates, designed to relieve stress and enhance pleasure. There are three triggers that release Endorphins—Eating, Connecting Socially, and Exercising. It's common knowledge that exercising releases this chemical in your brain that leads to feelings of happiness, even euphoria. But exercise isn't the only thing you can do to release endorphins. Smiling, eating certain foods, and even gossiping can do the trick.

According to *Wiki*, online reference source, there are many ways to harness our natural endorphins to help life's problems melt away. We can directly give ourselves an endorphin rush. The act of laughing stimulates the production of endorphins and helps us to feel good instantly. Laughter helps to relieve stress and has many other physical and emotional benefits.

- Laughing has so many therapeutic benefits that some people practice "laugh therapy" to schedule in some healthy laughter as often as possible.
- Sharing a joke with friends or finding something genuinely funny is the best way to make the most of laughter. Go for a deep, belly laugh that takes over your whole body.

True smiles, called *Duchenne smiles*, result in the production of endorphins, giving your mood a boost. A Duchenne smile is one that engages your entire face, including your eyes. It's almost impossible to fake and it only happens when you're feeling happy.

- A smile that engages just your mouth, and not your eyes, doesn't have the same beneficial effects.
- To boost your mood with a smile, try looking at pictures that make you smile, or talk to a person who makes you happy.

Studies show that gossiping stimulates pleasure centers in the brain and releases endorphins. Scientists believe that since we're social beings, gossip is developed as a way to stay connected, and we're rewarded for gossiping with an improved state of mind. Getting together with people and talking to our friends and family is a healthy act.
- Remember that gossip is the act of talking about other people, but it doesn't have to be negative in tone. Just updating your mom on what your brother has been up to, or cracking jokes about your uncle's antics, is a way to strengthen family bonds and improve your mood.

Helping yourself to a bowl of pasta with cheese, ice cream, or another carbohydrate-rich comfort food releases endorphins. People turn to these items during stressful moments because they really do make you feel better.

- You can enjoy *comfort* food without going off your diet. Try a bowl of old-fashioned oatmeal with a little honey and milk stirred in, or a plate of red beans and rice. You'll benefit from the carbohydrates without suffering from the consequences of eating refined carbohydrates.
- To elevate your mood even more, try pairing two endorphin stimulators together. Put some chocolate chips in your oatmeal, or add hot cayenne to your dish of pasta.

(references from wiki)

We also, live in an UNSEEN world or a SPIRITUAL world. This world even though we cannot see it is more real than and more powerful than the one we can see. Therefore, here is where the word EMOTIONS comes in to play.

Since we live in two worlds, *Human Sin* always has a dual source:

It has a supernatural source—where Satan and the principalities of the unseen world bring temptation. They plant thoughts and imaginations into our minds and hearts to cause us to walk away from God.

It has a human source—where we make wrong choices in response to the temptation, and not by the spirit of God. The 1970s *Flip Wilson Show's* female character, *Geraldine*— comedian *Flip Wilson* dressed in women's clothing, would click her fingers and say, "The devil made me do it." Well that is actually wrong, the devil can't make you do anything, without your choice.

Mixing senses, with emotions and endorphins, produces a carnal Christian. Who now even though loves the Lord, is caught up in being ON THE GRID, and lives a double life.

> James 1:5-8—If any of you lack wisdom, let him ask of God, that giveth to all men liberally, and upbraideth not, and it shall be given him. But let him ask in faith, nothing wavering. For he that wavereth is like a wave of the sea driven with the wind and tossed. For let not that man think that he shall receive any thing of the Lord. A double minded man is unstable in all his ways.

Emotions are things that change like the weather. We are up and feel good when things are going our way, when we hear good news, see good responses to things, share or post—on the Internet, read the newspaper, or engage social media. We have a great feeling when we eat or taste something that pleases our palate. When someone touches us gently, or holds our hand, we get all fuzzy and happy. These are all emotions, and they can and will cause problems. We seek these emotions because they makes us feel good.

However, emotions are unstable. Emotions are not bad. But, we should never be moved by emotions. However, there are several stories in the Bible where Jesus is moved with compassion.

> Matthew 9:36—But when he saw the multitudes, he was moved with compassion on them, because they fainted, and were scattered abroad, as sheep having no shepherd.

> Matthew 14:14—And Jesus went forth, and saw a great multitude, and was moved with compassion toward them, and he healed their sick.

Compassion differs from emotion and we do not mix the two. Compassion moves us to do something positive. Emotions can move us to make poor choices or poor decisions. Emotions move our body functions and our body suit, yet compassion moves something to change. Emotions come and go but the Word of God stays true forever.

Being OFF THE GRID, is not an emotional decision, but a spiritual decision. It's being in tune with God and walking in the Spirit. Emotions take us back to being ON THE GRID, because we desire pleasure and attention. Jesus was moved with compassion to do something for someone else. He did not look for fame or recognition, but to see others comforted and healed.

Many times as Christians, when someone comes to us with a problem, we make an assessment right then and there. We do not realize at that moment that, they could be in a life threatening situation or that your response could change the direction of that person's life forever.

Someone had asked me—what is the meaning of life? It's that all important question that I think everyone in the history of the world has desired to get an answer. So, I thought on it, prayed on it, and came up with this conclusion:

How do you relate to someone in their moment, when you're in your moment? The Answer, when two moments connect in the same moment there is a purpose. Then it becomes a Kairos moment in time. When we are consumed in our moment, and fail to look at the other person's moment, we miss the pleasure of being in God's moment.

Wow, now that is something to ponder on. Let me put it this way. In John, chapter 4, we see the story of the woman at the well. Jesus leaves Judea and departs to Galilee, but He sees the need to go through Samaria. The prompting of the Holy Spirit leads Him to Samaria instead of going directly to Galilee.

Notice, Jesus is being routed to a moment that is being designed to be a God moment. Jesus, being OFF THE GRID is listening to the directions from the Father. He comes to a city of Samaria, which is called Sychar, near Jacobs well. Now this woman is in her moment, and Jesus is in His moment. Remember when two moments collide it's a God moment, a Kairos moment in time, or a predetermined time. What happens next is all God.

> Jesus answered her, Whosoever drinketh of this water, shall thirst again.

Meaning drinking from a physical well of water. Remember we are talking about emotions, and our senses. Jesus is in the spirit speaking, yet she is in the flesh and the five senses—*Sight, Hearing, Touch, Taste,* and *Smell*. Now Jesus takes it out of emotions and into the spiritual realm. She is ON THE GRID, and Jesus is OFF THE GRID.

> John 4:13-14—But whosoever drinketh of the water that I shall give him shall never thirst; but the water that I shall give him shall be in him a well of water springing up into everlasting life.

We can see through this illustration that our emotions and our senses can get in the way of the spiritual discernment of God.

We look or express ourselves when someone is moody, sad, happy and glad. Depending on our frame of mind, we don't want them around, or tell them to get over it. We sometimes murmur under our breath, "They didn't deserve that" or "How come they got that when I have done more than them" or "It's not fair, look I have done all the work." When we are ON THE GRID, we are moved by emotions. When we are OFF THE GRID, we are moved with compassion not by emotions.

> In the book of Galatians, 5:22,23—But the fruit of the Spirit is love, joy, peace, longsuffering, gentleness, goodness, faith, meekness, temperance, against such there is no law.

These are all characteristics of someone who is OFF THE GRID. These characteristics cannot be obtained by anything you can do. You cannot buy them, earn them or barter them. You cannot trade for them, or bid on them. They are a gift to you and I, to be His hands extended to walk with the Lord.

> Hebrews 13:8—God's Word is true, Jesus Christ is the same yesterday, and today and forever, it changes not.

Emotions come and go, blow with the wind, and cause us to go up and down according to our input and input from others. Standing on the Word of God and knowing the Word of God will get us back to the presence of God and walk OFF THE GRID, and not desire the things of the flesh.

I don't want you to think that doing away with emotions or physical senses is what I am talking about. Let's look at emotions and being OFF THE GRID

In a later chapter we will be talking about The Presence of the Lord which will heighten your understanding of what I am sharing with you now.

How can the five senses that have been given to us by God be used for Spiritual things, to be used OFF THE GRID? When our physical body and our spirit are in tune with one another, it works to an advantage to see into the spiritual realm. The Bible tells us:

> 1 John 4:1— Beloved, believe not every spirit, but try (test) the spirits whether they are of God; because many false prophets are gone out into the world.
>
> 1 Corinthians 2:14—But the natural man receiveth not the things of the Spirit of God: for they are foolishness unto him, neither can he know them, because they are spiritually discerned.

When we are walking in the Spirit, and OFF THE GRID our five senses now are being used along with our spiritual discernment to be God's hands extended.

Sort of like being enhanced! Since we live in two worlds at the same time, we need to be in tune with the Spirit of God to make correct and disciplined decisions. The scriptures say that once we are born again, we become a new creature. A new creature which is **in** the world but not **of** the world. We live here, yet we have been transformed and relocated to a different address. We are just passing through. When we are ON THE GRID and walking in the flesh it becomes harder and harder to discern what is right and wrong because the flesh kicks in. The flesh wants things of this earth and the Spirit wants spiritual things—thus the battle.

> Romans 7:15-19—For that which I do I allow not: for what I would, that do I not, but what I hate, that do I. If then I do that which I would not, I consent unto the law that it is good. Now then it is no more I that do it, but sin that dwelleth in me. For I know that in me (that is in my flesh) dwelleth no good thing: for to will is present with me; but how to perform that which is good I find not. For the good that I would I do not: but the evil which I would not, that I do.

This is the dilemma. This is being ON THE GRID and OFF THE GRID. This is where the emotions come into play. Paul is saying, I want to do what is right, but I don't. There is a sin nature in me that wants to do that which is evil, and that is what I do.

Our senses can play tricks on us. Our senses with our emotions feed the sin nature in our lives and we go round and round on the roller coaster of life. This is why we need that break as Jesus took, that break to regroup and refocus, spend time alone with the Father and get on track to be OFF THE GRID.

Please consider at this time to take a break, meditate, seek the Father and allow the Holy Spirit to speak to you right now. Do it, right now, it could save your life.

Chapter Three
What Is Off The Grid?

Some of the films I used to watch as a kid seemed to be mostly about war, cowboys, adventure, and action pack movies. I guess I like a little excitement in my life. One of the shows was *Voyage to the Bottom of the Sea*.

The show was almost always filmed in a submarine. *Richard Baseheart* played the Captain and the submarine was called *Seaview*. Every episode they would come across some weird fish, or some huge mammal in the ocean. They would always come and save the day. I guess that is why I love these type of movies and TV programs.

From time to time, they would show a sonar screen, and you would hear *bleep, bleep, bleep* as the line would go around the screen. Sometimes they would turn off the sonar and become STEALTH. STEALTH is another word for invisible, or unnoticed. In those modes, the ship was not detected by another ship, or by anyone, because they were running silently in the water.

I would also watch war or airplane movies. In them, there was always someone in the tower or on the ground trying to detect an enemy aircraft that would be attacking by using radar. Radar and Sonar are very similar in purpose. They both are designed to DETECT and reveal, by a bleep on the screen if something is there. Sometimes aircraft would fly very low so as not be detected on screen until it was too late.

One such true incident was Pearl Harbor. The ships, aircraft, and soldiers were on the ground going about their everyday activity, not realizing that an enemy was already on their way to bomb, destroy, and steal the lives of many civilians and soldiers.

The Japanese airplanes flew across the ocean in secret, flying below the radar, in stealth mode, not making any sound or being noticed by anyone. Coming in below radar was a technique that allowed the Japanese to bomb and destroy much of Pearl Harbor. The conclusion, "A day that will live in infamy", announced President Franklin Roosevelt, on that tragic day.

What was the Japanese tactic? They were OFF THE GRID. Hence, the title of this book. Learning how to walk in the Spirit and be not detected by the enemy is part of being a sold out, warrior for Jesus Christ. In the following chapter, we will discuss how many of the Men of God in the Bible learned this mode of travel. We should as well as we "see the day approaching".

Genesis 22:1-14 is most likely a story we have all grown up hearing over and over. A story of a father (Abraham) and a son (Isaac).

OFF THE GRID — ERIC G. ZEIDLER

> And it came to pass after these things, that God did tempt Abraham, and said unto him, Abraham, and he said, Behold here I am. And he said, Take now thy son, thine only son Issac whom thou lovest, and get thee into the land Moriah, and offer him there for a burnt offering upon one of the mountains which I will tell thee of.

Not only did God tell him to take his son to offer up as a sacrifice, but God also, told him to walk, and I will show you where to go.

This is not new to Abraham, in Chapter 12, we read:

> Now the Lord had said unto Abram, (notice he didn't pass God's test yet, so God didn't call him Abraham) Get thee out of thy country, and from thy kindred, and from thy father's house, unto a land that I will shew thee.

And then God explains to him that if YOU ARE OBEDIENT, then here is your reward.

> (and I will) make thy name great, thou shalt be a blessing.

Abram learned early about being OFF THE GRID, listening to God, and him alone. I'm sure that his family had many questions. "Where are we going? Why are we going? Our family is here. I can't leave the family. How will you make a living? And, where will we live?" God says in Hebrews that He counted it as righteousness to him.

Being OFF THE GRID, is not only being obedient to God but willing to take orders and listen to His exact plan. Not our plans, our agenda, or our ideas, but His. How many times do we come up with a plan and tell God here it is? And expect God to say, "Oh, okay." His plans are much greater and bigger than anything within our thinking.

Back to Abraham and Isaac—Offering up Isaac and obediently going where God said He would reveal is being NOT ON RADAR. You see the enemy uses our words, our actions, and our murmuring to figure out what to do to stop, hinder, or oppose God's plan. The enemy wants us to stop thinking about what God wants. God desires our absolute obedience and presence to get us through.

Abraham and Isaac have traveled up the mountain that God said to go. They have all the necessary items, wood, sticks, and fire starters to make Isaac into that sacrifice. The scripture continues.

> 22:5—And Abraham said unto his young men, Abide ye hwith the ass, and I and the lad will go yonder and worship, and come again to you.
>
> 22:6— And Abraham took the wood of the burnt offering, and laid it upon Isaac his son, and he took the fire in his hand, and a knife, and they went both of them together.
>
> 22:7—And Isaac spake unto Abraham his father, and said, My father: and he said Here am I, my son. And he said, Behold the fire and the wood: but where is the lamb for a burnt offering.

Notice that the first thing on Abraham's mind is WORSHIP—getting into the presence of the Almighty God. Worship here is obedience. This is the first time that Isaac questions his father. After all, I'm sure he is getting a little nervous?

22:8 And Abraham said, (KEY WORDS), My son, God will PROVIDE HIMSELF a lamb for a burnt offering: so they went both of then together:

TRUST and OBEDIENCE are fundamental for being OFF THE GRID. When we become focused on us, and our way of thinking, we cannot operate in the Spiritual realm or understand God's way of thinking. FAITH now comes into play. When we are ON THE GRID, we become so spiritually numb that our spiritual discernment yields to poor choices or fleshly decisions.

The final part of this story is that of faith:

22:13—And Abraham lifted up his eyes, and looked, and behold behind him a ram caught in a thicket by his horns: and Abraham went and took the ram, and offered him up for a burnt offering in the stead of his son.

Is God good or what?

Abraham was STEALTH, not knowing where God was taking him, not posting on social media about what was going on, not sharing with anyone else, but just being still and knowing that HE IS GOD. The whole time Abraham and Isaac are not visible, not on the radar of the enemy. WHY? Because obedience is about being still and doing what God has asked you to do. The reward is from HIM and HIM alone. In this world of being popular, being famous, or in the spotlight, PUTS US right on the radar screen. I have learned over these past years that the more I am out of the spotlight, the more I can do for the Kingdom of God. When I start to reveal what God is doing, the enemy seems to be right there trying to figure out a road block, a wall, or a way to destroy God's plan. Just like the Japanese military attack of Pearl Harbor, their goal—STEALTH, not noticed, invisible, and undetected by anyone. So, when they hit, they hit hard.

When we are listening to the Holy Spirit, we are OFF THE GRID of the flesh and the world. Then we can start to hear every leading and every plan that God has for us. The goal—so we can be there for God's next moment in time with someone else. We miss the major blessings because we fall into the same trap day after day, week after week, and month after month. We've been in the same rut we have been in for a long time. When we are ready, prayed up, available, and purposeful, the Lord will sometimes say, NOT HERE but GO THERE, and we need to be ready. That's another way of being OFF THE GRID. An example of this is found in the book of Acts.

In chapter 16 of the Acts of the Apostles, we see Paul, Silas, and soon to follow Timotheus traveling as they preach in many different cities. Here is an example of being STEALTH and OFF THE GRID.

> Acts 16:6—Now when they had gone throughout Phrygia and the region of Galatia, and were forbidden of the Holy Ghost to preach the word to Asia,
>
> Acts 16:7—After they were come to Mysis, they assayed to go into Bithynia; BUT THE SPIRIT suffered them not."
>
> Acts 16:8— And they passing by Mysis came down to Troas.
>
> Acts 16:9—And a vision appeared to Paul in the night; There stood a man of Macedonia, and prayed him, saying, Come over into Macedonia and help us.

Acts 16:10 And after he had seen the vision, IMMEDIATELY, we endeavored to go into Macedonia assuredly gathering that the Lord had called us for to preach the gospel unto them.

They are now in God's moment, their plans have been CHANGED, their plans have been ALTERED. They are walking in STEALTH waiting for what God has for them. They were willing to change their plans for God's plan. No pride, no judgment, no one sharing their input, GOD IS SPEAKING they ANSWERED. What was the results?

Acts 16:14— And a certain woman named Lydia, a seller of purple, of the city of Thyatira, which worshipped God, heard us: whose heart the Lord opened, that she attended unto the things which were spoken of Paul.

Acts 16:15 —And when she was baptized, and her household....

The greatest blessing, we can ever receive from God is being His hands extended and seeing lives changed right before our eyes. Here is that example. If Paul, Silas and Timotheus did not listen, but followed their agenda, they would have missed a MOMENT WITH GOD.

The enemy is seeking and searching those who are ON THE GRID.

1 Peter 5:8—Be sober, be vigilant, because your adversary the devil, as a roaring lion, walketh about, seeking whom he may devour:

In a herd of wildebeests if you are injured or hurting, you don't want to wonder outside the pack where you become visible. You stay inside the pack where the predator can't see the difference between those that are small, medium, large, or those that are hurting or weak.

The predator is seeking whom he may devour, those that are weak. The more we are ON THE GRID and VISIBLE the more we become vulnerable to the predator. When we open ourselves up to social media, we open ourselves up to hurt, attacks, and problems, because like the enemy is as a roaring lion, a predator, seeking whom he may devour.

> Proverbs 3:5, 6—Trust in the Lord with all thine heart; and lean not unto your own understanding, In all your ways acknowledge him, and he shall direct thy paths.

If the Japanese fighter planes were just a little bit higher flying, our radar would have picked them up, and we would not have lost so many men, women, planes or ships during the attack on Pearl Harbor. How do we win the battle against Satan?—fly OFF THE GRID. Jesus is the best example we can use, and I wanted to save this until the end of the chapter to show the importance of this topic—OFF THE GRID.

In the New Testament, there are six stories that Jesus heals people, and he shares with them, my paraphrase, I'm—OFF THE GRID, "tell no one." Here are the examples of Jesus, our mentor.

Example #1 There is a man who is a leper who asks Jesus to make him clean.

> Matthew 8:4—And Jesus saith unto him, See thou tell no man; but go thy way, shew thyself to the priest, and offer the gift that Moses commanded, for a testimony unto them.

Though Jesus is the Messiah, the Lord, He still had to obey the law that was written for cleanliness. He didn't want the recognition or praise, but that God would be glorified.

> Leviticus 13:3—And the priest shall look on the plague in the skin of the flesh: and when the hair in the plague in turned white, and the plague in sight be deeper than the skin of his flesh it is a plague of leprosy: and the priest shall look on him, and pronounce him unclean."

> Leviticus 13:6—And the priest shall look on him again the seventh day: and behold, if the plague be somewhat dark, and the plague spread not in the skin, the priest shall pronounce him clean: It is but a scab: and he shall wash his clothes, and be clean.

Example #2 Jesus finished telling Peter that he is hearing from God. Jesus declares to him that he was correct in saying that "Thou art Christ, the Son of the living God." Upon that revelation, Jesus now gives Peter the keys to the kingdom. Then—

> Matthew 16:20 —Then charged he his disciples that they should tell no man that he was Jesus the Christ.

Isn't it amazing, as we see over these scriptures that the battle we fight is against the enemy. As a warrior for Christ, we don't need to expose the battle plan from God.

Just like being in a military war today, we would not send the plans of the attack to the enemy. Likewise, we should not expose the plan and purposes of God in our lives.

Example #3 Jesus heals a blind and dumb man. Jesus put his fingers in the man's ears, spits on his tongue, and the man could hear and see.

> Mark 7:36 —And he charged them that they should tell no man: but the more he charged them, so much the more a great deal they published it:

Even Jesus had problems with no one listening. Everyone around was walking ON THE GRID, walking in amazement, and talking all about the miracles that were happening in front of their eyes. Jesus wanted to be used by God, and not let the attention or attraction get into the way of being STEALTH.

Example #4 Jesus heals another blind man on the side of the road.

> Mark 8:26—And he sent him away to his house, saying, Neither go into the town, nor tell it to any in the town.

Example #5 Jesus takes Peter, John, and James with him to a mountain top. There before their very eyes, he appears in brilliant white raiment, with Moses and Elijah. The disciples are in awe in what they are experiencing. They even want to build three tabernacles to remember this event. But Jesus says—

> And as they came down from the mountain, he charged them that they should tell no man what things they had seen, till the Son of man were risen from the dead. Mark 9:9

Jesus knew his time was short; he also knew that his fame and presence was starting to become well known. He wanted so much to be able to operate in STEALTH—OFF THE GRID, where he had the most lives touched.

Example #6 Jesus goes into a house of a ruler of the synagogue whose daughter is dead. He asked for Jesus to touch her.

> Luke 8:56—And her parents were astonished; but he charged them that they should tell no man what was done.

Here you have it, several examples to consider what it means to operate in STEALTH and OFF THE GRID.

Several years ago, I had the opportunity to go to a pastor's breakfast in Toms River NJ. There was a man of God, a native American Indian, speaking at this breakfast. Pastors from all over New Jersey came. He was a representative from the Indian nation as well as a representative in Washington DC. He said something that has stuck with me for several years. Now every time, I go to a place to preach, speak, or share I consider what he said.

He said, We in America force our opinion on others like vomiting on someone. We speak and do not care if we are asked. We share when it is not our turn. We give our opinion even though someone hasn't asked for it.

He continued, "In the Indian Heritage, we ask the person we are speaking to—first, to give us permission to speak into their life." Wow, what a comment, asking first before we give our opinion. What a novel idea that is. Isn't that what Jesus did? He never forced His thoughts on anyone else.

We have lost a lot of proper respect, and consideration for others. Being OFF THE GRID will attempt to restore God's design for our lives. We need a change now in America, in our lives, but it has to start first with us. Time is short. We who desire to make it to the end must change our heart and attitude towards those around us.

OFF THE GRID is not seeing the bleep on the radar screen. OFF THE GRID is being so silent and still that we can work without anyone noticing. OFF THE GRID is being in the presence and obedience of God not just on Sunday, but every day. OFF THE GRID is a choice. You can choose life today! Go ahead—take a step of FAITH. YOU CAN DO IT!

> Philippians 4:13—I can do all things through Christ which strengthened me."

Chapter Four
Being the Voice Not the Echo

Matthew 3:3—For this is he that was spoken of by the prophet Isaiah, saying, The voice of one crying in the wilderness, Prepare ye the way of the Lord, make his paths straight.

Luke 4:18—The Spirit of the Lord is upon me, because he hath anointed me to preach the gospel to the poor; he hath sent me to heal the brokenhearted, to preach deliverance to the captives, and recovering of sight to the blind, to set at liberty them that are bruised, to preach the acceptable year of the Lord.

Traveling around the United States and into Europe, I have had the opportunity to see many sights. Many that were spectacular, elegant, and beautiful. Some not attractive, but having a unique appeal. The ones that I always remember are the ones that speak to me.

Growing up, as I shared in Chapter One, about camping on my birthday, we went to the *Blue Ridge Mountains* in the *Shenandoah Valley* in *Virginia* one year. My family and I went into the *Luray Caverns*, a spectacular view about 60 feet underground. I remember that trip in my mind from that day until now. Most recently, in August of 2015, my wife Jaimie and I returned to the foothills of the same place. It brought back many memories, except this time we went to the *Shenandoah Caverns*. On this trip, I was already preparing this book. When we went through the caverns, the Lord showed me the title of this chapter as an example I was about to see.

We had a young man about nineteen or twenty who was our guide. He was very informative because he grew up in the caverns. His father was the manager. After getting into an elevator that would only take eight people, at a time, down the narrow shaft, to the cavern floor, the group I was with, about 18, waited together until it was time to travel as a team through the caverns. The place was awesome. He shared, how two boys found a cold opening in the ground and decided to dig the hole bigger and go onto a journey to wherever it took them. I can imagine, just a flashlight and hanging on a rope, what they saw. It would remind me of an Indiana Jones movie.

After traveling for about thirty minutes, we came to the bottom and center of the caverns which was about two-hundred feet down. The young guide made an announcement and it ECHOED through the caverns. "Stay to the right!" There were some awesome colored parts of the cave right where we were, but he directed us to stay over to the right.

There was another group coming back, and he wanted to make room for them. All but two adults and three kids listened. I watched as the group tried to pass while the two adults and three kids where in their way. The adults were busy taking pictures. The kids where not even paying attention and were very disruptive. The group passed, and the guide made another announcement, that ECHOED, "If you would like to take some pictures at this time, please go ahead."

As I was standing there, it was if God was saying to me, "See them over there they are ON THE GRID." I laughed to myself and followed the group around the caverns some more. As we followed the group the three kids became more and more disruptive, and the two adults seemed like they could not handle them in this environment. Then, it came to me—*being the voice and not the echo.* The kids were listening to the adults and watching them. They were not paying attention to the young man who knew all about the caverns. They were being taught how to be ON THE GRID. It was all about them. The rules didn't apply to them. I am sure if there was an emergency, they would have been the first to panic.

The VOICE has power, but the ECHO does not. Have you ever been in a place like a tunnel, a fort or a valley, and when you yell it echoes, and echoes, and echoes what you say?

Not far from where I live, there is a place called Fort Mott, an old Civil War fort with rooms that are dark and spooky. As kids, we would run through them, stand right in front of someone, touch them, or yell, and watch them jump and scream. If you get lost in a place like that, you would yell, "WHERE ARE YOU", and a voice would echo back, "RIGHT HERE". You would repeat that over and over until you moved closer and closer to the real VOICE and not the ECHO.

> John 10:4-5—And when he putteth forth his own sheep, he goeth before them, and the sheep follow him: for they know his voice. And a stranger will they not follow, but will flee from him; for they know not the voice of strangers.

We have so many voices that are all around us. They sound good. They sound truthful. They even look right. Yet the truth, God wants us to hear the true VOICE and not an ECHO that is not real. As a pastor I tell my congregation—

> John 14:26 —But the Comforter, which is the Holy Ghost (Spirit) whom the Father (God) will send in my name, he shall teach you all things, and bring all things to your remembrance, whatsoever I have said unto you.

The true voice is the voice of the Holy Spirit of God that will lead us, guide us, and show us the way to the Savior. When we are ON THE GRID, and we don't take time to listen for the true voice, the voice of the Holy Spirit, we miss out on that intimacy with the Father. Later in the book we will share and help you find that *Presence of the Lord*.

Several years ago there was a famous singing group that made millions of records and dollars, touring all over, by lip-syncing all their songs. They were not using their voice, but using the echo from a recording. They lost a tremendous amount of respect and trust after the news was released by the media.

Another mark of being OFF THE GRID is knowing and hearing GOD's voice. We cannot hear His voice if we are ON THE GRID. It may sound like HIM. It may even look like HIM, but is it a copy or an original? The enemy knows how to mimic attempting to replicate the movements of God. The Word says—

> And no marvel; for Satan himself is transformed into an angel of light. —2 Corinthians 11:14

When we are ON THE GRID, Satan, and his principalities, can even look like it is a God thing. They can transform the very tools in front of you and make you believe. That is why this book is being written. In the last days the Word says:

> 2 Timothy 3:1-5— This know also, that in the last days perilous times shall come. For men shall be lovers of their own selves, covetous, boasters, proud, blasphemers, disobedient to parents, unthankful, unholy, without natural affections, trucebreakers, false accusers, incontinent, fierce, despisers of those that are good, Traitors, heady, high-minded, lovers of pleasure more than lovers of God; Having a form of godliness, but denying the power thereof: from such turn away.

These are examples of being ON THE GRID. We become so caught up in ourselves we do not hear the still small voice (1 Kings 19:12) anymore, but listen to the echoes of those around us.

Being OFF THE GRID, is stop reading other people's devotionals, books, and magazines as the only source for getting the truth. It becomes very easy to read what someone else has researched so you do not have to spend the time doing it yourself.

> Isaiah 55:6—Seek ye the Lord while he may be found, call ye upon him while he is near".
>
> Psalms 63:1—O God, thou art my God; early will I seek thee;

We need to stop watching Christian television, TV specials about Jesus, or Jesus movies as our only way of getting the Word. If you do not read the Word on a daily basis and let the Holy Spirit lead you, guide you in all truth, then where will truth come from? It will come from the echo but the echo has no power. It is not the real thing. When we read the Word for our-understanding, the Holy Spirit chisels it in our heart so that we might not sin.

What happens when an alcoholic, drug user, food abuser, or anyone with an addiction, comes to you and ask you to help them get what they need? If you give them what they want, you become an enabler. Someone who continues to feed their addiction. We can become dysfunctional by listening to everyone preaching every kind of theology, topic, or sermon. If we don't search it out for ourselves, we become an addict to the echo and start to decline instead of growing. We actually allow these types of media to enable us NOT to read the Word of God for ourselves. We believe we are growing in truth, but actually are stunting our growth, due to others influencing our lifestyle. Thus we become dysfunctional in our own spiritual way.

By being OFF THE GRID, God has given each one of us the opportunity to HEAR from Him. He is asking us to be the VOICE and not the ECHO. We desire to be His hands extended, but we get lazy, instead of searching for ourselves, we listen to others and form our spiritual truths by what others say. When we get a revelation from someone else's writings or teaching, we claim it as our own revelation.

Someone else's revelation is an ECHO. We repeat that as truth as if we first received it. There is nothing wrong with hearing and receiving someone else's knowledge. The Scripture says *there is wisdom in the multitude of council*. However, when we rely on that continually for truth in our life, we are already being deceived. We think we are growing but need more and more information from others to feed that addiction.

Being the VOICE is a little like a serpent and a dove. Jesus is about to send his disciples (Apostles) out to preach, to heal and be His hands extended.

Matthew 10:16—Behold I send you forth as sheep in the midst of wolves: be ye therefore WISE as serpents, and harmless as doves".

First we see Jesus warning them that THEY WILL come under attack. You would never send sheep into a pack of wolves unless you knew the outcome. Jesus knew that they would be protected from the elements of human nature. That nature of hatred, jealousy, death, and destruction. The disciples may not have seen or known what was about to happen in their lives, but that is where the VOICE gives us comfort.

Wise as a serpent is the illustration of how a serpent (snake) attacks its prey. Remember we are talking about WISDOM. When I see a snake the first thing I think about is cold and slimy. My skin crawls. The analogy here is not based upon what the serpent looks like, but his wisdom.

When we see a snake, they are usually in a coil position. That position is for a purpose. First, if they are in a coil, it is easier to protect himself. When they are stretched out, they become very vulnerable to attack and to be eaten or killed. Preservation is their first part of wisdom. Second, in a coiled position they can strike at a moment's notice. Striking also allows them to extend themselves several times in length. They sit and wait. They are quiet, still, and purposeful. Just like being OFF THE GRID, they are undetected and under the radar.

When Jaimie and I first moved into the house we live in, which had been sitting for about four years, there were times I had to go down into the crawlspace and cellar to do some repairs. One day, while walking around the cellar, cleaning cobwebs and looking around, I came about three feet from a black snake coiled on the dirt, quiet, still, and waiting. It wasn't going to attack, unless provoked. At first, it frightened me, but he did nothing. The snake was not scared. He was not frightened by me. The snake was confident in who and where he was. It wasn't until I grabbed a rake and extended it towards him that he struck at the rake. (Incidentally, I did get him along with four others out of the cellar before we moved in.)

Being OFF THE GRID, we wait on God. We are still before God. We prepare for what God has for us. Yet, when it is time to share the Gospel, we pray, travel, and go where He wants us to go. We launch out like the snake does, to make a difference in others' lives. Notice the snake after he strikes, he recoils back to the same position as if nothing ever happened. The WISDOM of the snake is not to be open to attack once he strikes. After we hear from God and are obedient, we regroup and get ready for the next assignment from Him.

BEING HARMLESS AS DOVES

A dove is a little bit different in the way they move. A dove is as quiet as a snake but flies AWAY when a noise or motion comes near them. They react almost without a whisper—gentle, beautiful and harmless. OFF THE GRID as a dove, is like not letting things get you down, avoiding controversy, or people telling you what to do. We avoid drama. We fly from those who cause us hurt. We fly gently away to a place of solace and peace in the arms of God. Many of the problems in our lives are due to our actions. Opposition sometimes is caused by ourselves wanting to stay and fight a battle that is not ours in the first place.

1 Samuel 17: 47—And all this assembly shall know that the LORD saveth not with sword and spear: for the battle is the LORD's and he will give you into our hands".

When we stay in that battle, we whine, cry, and feel depressed. With the wisdom of a snake, and the harmless response of a dove, we recoil and strike when the Holy Spirit says, and then fly away to live another day. Being the VOICE and not the ECHO is walking in humility.

Philippians 2:8 —And being found in fashion as a man, he humbled himself, and became obedient unto death, even the death of the cross.

1 Peter 5:5—Likewise, ye younger, submit yourselves unto the elder. Yea, all of you be subject one to another, and be clothed with humility: for God resisteth the proud, and giveth grace to the humble.

I was told this saying years ago, "All that and a box of chocolates and a bag of chips", paraphrased, I am all about myself. When we are the ECHO, we are all about ourselves. We want to hear ourselves talk, comment, express opinions, and be in charge. An ECHO does not have any power. It is a replica of something that has power. An ECHO is harmless and weak. An ECHO is PRIDE.

Revelation 12:11—And they overcame him (Satan) by the blood of the Lamb (Jesus) and by the word of their testimony: and they loved not their lives unto the death.

An ECHO is someone else's testimony. WE OVERCOME by *our* testimony. Over the years, God has taken us in many different direction and many different places. We have a lot of testimonies and have witnessed many testimonies. There are many believers in the Body of Christ that never share or do not have a testimony. We use someone else's testimony to share.

Nine years ago, in August of 2006, I was diagnosed with oral cancer. God has healed me, and I am cancer free. I wrote a book entitled, *Silence of the Tongue*, which is my testimony of how God used the sixteen and half hour operation, and ten days in the hospital, to teach me a valuable lesson on UNITY. The book has now been in the second printing, and many believers and non-believers have read the book and lives have been changed. That's being the VOICE, not an ECHO. When we share our life experiences, we can give from the heart.

Being the VOICE, being OFF THE GRID, and not letting our EMOTIONS control us are all part of living a life of freedom in the Spirit. It's walking in joy, peace and righteousness here on earth. In this world of confusion, stress, hatred, bitterness, doubt, and un-forgiveness all around, we need to learn to get into the presence of God. In order to do that, it requires going back to the simpler things in life, and regain the peace and joy we all long for. Admit it, the roller coaster ride gets old fast. The quiet ride on the lake is needed more often. Both of my books, *Silence of the Tongue* and *OFF THE GRID*, have been written when I was away by myself, at the New Jersey shore, where I desire to be in HIS PRESENCE.

Jesus was good at that:

Matthew 14:22, 23—And straightway Jesus constrained his disciples to get into a ship, and to go before him unto the other side, while he sent the multitudes away. And when he sent the multitudes away, he went up into a mountain apart to pray; and when the evening was come he was there alone.

OFF THE GRID ERIC G. ZEIDLER

BREAK TIME, to be the VOICE. Even Jesus had to get away—to be still, to be quiet, to be in that coil, preparing to strike, preparing as God restored Him, and gave Him new directions. Most of all, He needed to be in the presence of His Father, Father God.

I pray that you are starting to see how we as a generation have gone way too far. We have learned to play church, and play being a Christian. We have even learned how to act, and react as a Christian should. Concurrently, we have denied that deep down inside, there is an emptiness, a void, something missing? We have been ON THE GRID too long, on the merry-go-round too long, on the journey around the mountain too long. We have read every how-to-book, every spiritual book on this, and that, yet as the scripture proclaims in Revelations 2:2-4.—

> I know thy works, and thy labour, and thy patience, and how thou canst not bear them which are evil; and thou hast tried them which say they are apostles and are not, and hast found them liars: And hast borne, and hast patience, and for my names sake hast laboured, and hast not fainted. Nevertheless, I have somewhat against thee, because thou hast left thy first love.

So, today is the day of Salvation—regain your position in the Kingdom of God, pull up your boot straps, snug your belt on, and fight the good fight of faith. You're needed now more than ever. As we see the time approaching, God is looking for a few people who are willing to be the VOICE and not the ECHO.

OFF THE GRID   ERIC G. ZEIDLER

Chapter Five
The Presence Of The Lord

There is nothing that compares to the experience of a visitation from the Lord.

> Exodus 25: 8—And let them make me a sanctuary that I may dwell among them".
>
> Exodus 33: 9—And it came to pass, as Moses entered into the tabernacle, the cloudy pillar descended and stood at the door of the tabernacle, and the LORD talked with Moses.
>
> 1 Corinthians 3:16,17—Know ye not that ye are the temple of the God, and that the Spirit of God dwelleth in you? If any man defiles the temple of God, him shall God destroy; for the temple of God is holy, which temple ye are.

On one of my trips to Romania, with Pastor Eric Norton from Delaware, was to be a very special experience for me in how to experience the presence of God in a tangible way. When I say tangible, I mean feeling the presence of the cloudy pillar as described in Exodus 33:9.

We were staying and helping out in the canteens and the orphanages that we went to each time we traveled to Romania. The canteens were a place where the children who were needy, poor or did not have a place to eat would come. We would go and help serve. We share Bible stories and use puppets to explain the Gospel in a childlike way. The children were taught how to dance—not just ordinary dancing, but Hebrew traditional dances. They loved to dance for hours. Sometimes they would dance so long that the soup and food would get cold, and we would have to stop. It was as if they had no cares at all. Can you imagine what our church services would be like if we just came in to dance with freedom and not worry about any of our cares?

This one trip, all of the children from the orphanages and canteens were going to put on a show at one of the largest venues in the city. It was once a communistic theater where they would have rallies and meetings for the top leaders of the city. The day of the performance, all the children were ready. The girls had on beautiful gowns and the boys were all dressed to the nines. The story line of the dancing told the Bible story of Adam and Eve. The children were excited and nervous. The theater was packed. People all over the city were there. The lights go down. The show begins.

The children were flawless. Almost at the end of the performance, the children grabbed hands and formed three circles on stage. A large one, and smaller one, and another one inside for the smaller children. What was about to happen, and no one knew, was that God was about to make a public appearance. The song started slowly, and the words went like this:

Off The Grid — Eric G. Zeidler

The Lord is building Jerusalem,
The Lord is building Jerusalem,
Gathering together the outcast of Israel,
Healing broken hearts,
Binding up their wounds,
The Lord is building,
The Lord is building up Jerusalem.

It started to go faster and faster. Every circle going into the opposite direction. The gowns were flowing. The children were smiling. All of a sudden, the air started to get smoky, and dense, and tears started to run down the children's faces.

Then many who were up front started to cry and started to kneel down in the aisles, as God's presence started to flow all over the building. This moment went on for about twenty-five minutes, and the song ended with a serious clapping and praising Jesus. The children and those in the circles started looking at the audience and one another saying, "What just happened?"

After the concert, the children boarded the vans. We met back at the orphanage where they changed and got ready for dinner. Pastor Eric and I had a chance to see some of the older children before dinner to tell them how great they did on stage, at the theater. A group of about four or five sat around us and asked, "Why did we start crying during the last song?" We shared with them that the presence of God was in the room, and when the presence of God is in the room, the physical body cannot bear emotionally the Love of the Almighty God. That is the presence we can have every day, when we are "OFF THE GRID". Those children were so innocent, so wanting to be the very best they could, working together as a team, and desiring to please the Lord,

> Psalms 66:8—O bless our God, ye people, and to the voice of his praise to be heard:
>
> Psalms 100:4—Enter into his gates with thanksgiving and into his courts with praise: be thankful unto him, and bless his name.

To understand walking and being in the presence of the Lord, we have to take a journey back to the Old Testament. There with Adam in the Garden and Moses in the wilderness we see the desire of God wanting us to be in His presence on a daily basis.

> Genesis 3:8—And they heard the voice of the LORD God walking in the garden in the cool of the day.

We see that Adam and Eve would walk in the Garden of Eden with God and talk to Him on a daily basis. Can you imagine no sin, no problems, no issues in life, plenty to eat, and NO STRESS?

Yes, I would say that was paradise. However, we know that Adam was disobedient to the Word that God told them about eating from the tree of the Knowledge of Good and Evil. Although Eve ate first, Adam was the one with the Spiritual authority. Adam should have told Eve— "No, I cannot eat of that tree less we would surely die."

Fast forward a few thousand years, and Moses is on the scene ready to free the Hebrews from four-hundred years of being in bondage to Egypt. God throughout the generations is looking for a people who will worship Him and desire to be like Adam and Eve before the fall, walking and communicating with Him.

> Exodus 25: 21, 22—And thou shalt put the mercy seat above upon the ark, and in the ark thou shalt put the testimony that I shall give thee. And there I will meet with thee, and I will commune with thee from above the mercy seat.

Here is a representation of God's mercy. He says that "His mercy is new every morning." So, in His presence there is Mercy, and in His presence, we meet Him there. Let's look at the difference from being ON THE GRID and OFF THE GRID in this situation.

> Matthew 5:16—Let your light so shine before men, that they may see your good works, and glorify your Father which is in heaven".

In order for us to glorify God, and to be in His presence we need to be OFF THE GRID, not being notice, so the world and others would see our good works, and glorify God. When we are in His presence, our desire is to see Jesus be lifted up and God being glorified. We desire to be a vessel of His Grace and a conduit to be used by Him. If we desire anything outside of that formula, we are operating ON THE GRID—we, and our selfish desires are going to be noticed.

How do we get into His presence?

Again, we need to go back to the illustration that God gave to Moses in the wilderness. He was told to construct a tabernacle based on the tabernacle God showed him on the mountain. That tabernacle was in heaven. So, the tabernacle on earth is a replica of the tabernacle in heaven. Since the tabernacle in heaven is the sovereign model, then from it we can glean insight on entering into God's presence—like the priest did when they would enter in, once a year, to sacrifice for the people.

When you entered into the court yard, there were two pieces of furniture, modeling the first part of entering in to God's presence. Realize, this is not a formula. It is an example of what the high priest had to do to enter the *Holy of Holies* where God would meet him there.

The first piece was the *brazen alter*—one large square piece with four horns, on the corners, for the blood to be placed. The burnt offering was placed there to be burnt, as a sacrifice. We are called to be a living sacrifice in the New Testament. So, *the first step* is *being willing* to get OFF THE GRID, and sacrifice our time, our lives, our heart and our plans to Him.

The second piece before going into the inner court was a *brazen laver*. This looked like a huge bird bath, but was made of gold, and was beaten on the inside to look almost mirror-like. This was full of water, to look into it was to see the reflection of yourself or your sin. Here, you would wash your hands symbolizing being washed clean. The *second step* is *repentance*. Looking into our everyday life, our past and present sin, and asking God to forgive us of our short comings.

Before you enter the *inner court*, you now have given over your life to God, and have asked for repentance from your sins. Now you enter into the inner court. On the right, is *the table of showbread* which is *the third piece*. The priest would make fresh bread each Sabbath, which represent Jesus as the *Bread of Life*. So, the *third step* is *fellowship with Jesus*—eating of the bread, which is the Word or Bread of Life.

The fourth piece is *the candlestick*, which was attended to every day, by filling the lampstand with oil and not letting it run out. This was the only light in the tabernacle. Therefore, *the forth step* is *understanding that the Word is a lamp unto my feet and a light unto my path* as it says in

Psalms 119:105. The Word guides us in the right direction by the power of the Holy Spirit.

The fifth piece is *the altar of incense*, which burned continually, twenty-four hours a day, seven days a week, as a sweet incense to God. This was right outside *the veil*, which was latched together with straps and only had an opening in the bottom to gain access. So, *the fifth step* is *our prayer time*, as the prayers of the saints are always going up to God as a sweet incense which pleases the Lord.

 In Summary—
Brazen Alter—Giving our lives to Him
Being OFF THE GRID, our time, talents, and gifts to HIM.
Brazen Laver—Looking at your life
Reflecting on the sin that is in our lives, and repenting
Table of Shewbread—Representation of Jesus
Reading and allowing the Word to change our lives
Candlestick—Oil and the Light
Listening to the Holy Spirit who guides our steps
Alter of Incense—Smoke going up to God

Now if we are doing all of these things on a daily basis, we are one step closer to being OFF THE GRID and in the presence of the Lord. So many times we show up on Sunday and think we can just casually walk right into the service, sit down, and God just shows up. It's true, we bring the Holy Spirit in with us, because He is in us. Remember still, God cannot reside in the presence of SIN. If we can concentrate on living our lives each day OFF THE GRID, we can enter into His presence more often and more intense.

The next step is being able to enter into the HOLY OF HOLIES, where God told Moses that He would meet him there. Wow, when I look at this over and over, I see a promise that God gives each and every one of us. Summarizing the KEY to being OFF THE GRID— Getting rid of EMOTIONS, BEING THE VOICE and not the ECHO, and getting rid of or dying to self.

> Luke 9:25 ASV—For what is a man profited, if he gained the whole world, and lose or forfeit his own self?

We can have it all—cars, house, money, fame, friends, family, a great job, lots of children and even a great church, but if we don't have the intimate relationship with our Lord and Savior Jesus Christ, we have nothing.—Amen

> Matthew 7:23—And then will I profess unto them, I never knew you, depart from me, ye that work iniquity.

"I NEVER KNEW YOU." Can you imagine? You have a friend growing up. The two of you become distant through the years. One day you're somewhere and you meet up again. You introduce your longtime friend to your spouse and they turn around and say, "WHO ARE YOU?" Wow, what a shock that would be. Yet, Jesus will do the same to those who are caught up in themselves, worldly, and ON THE GRID.

I know this is a strong chapter, but it is very much needed in the Body of Christ.

God wants to restore the intimacy with Him. God wants to walk in the cool of the morning with us again. God wants us to stop and smell the roses with Him. God wants us to spend more time with Him. And,

God wants more of you than ever before. Are you willing to give HIM YOUR ALL?

Acts 4:12—Matthew 16:20Neither is there salvation in any other: for there is none other name under heaven given among men, whereby we must be saved.

OFF THE GRID   ERIC G. ZEIDLER

Chapter Six
Why We Need To Get Off The Grid

THE MARRIAGE SUPPER

The message within this chapter, I believe, will open up your heart and cause you to see the need to get OFF THE GRID and get back into the presence of the Lord. The things discussed are all around us. Therefore, the purpose of this chapter is not to be a scare tactic, but an eye-opening realization of where all are in the Body of Christ right now. I believe, as we examine these things, it will bring open-heart revelation, highlighting the need to get OFF THE GRID and get back into the presence of God.

Remember, the scriptures that I use are coming from Jesus himself. These are warnings, and yet words of comfort, to help us get OFF THE GRID and daily into His Word and presence.

The subtitle of this chapter is, *The Marriage Supper*.

Matthew 7:13 - 14 Enter ye in at the strait gate; for wide is the gate, and broad is the way, that leadeth to destruction, and many there be which go in there at: Because strait is the gate and narrow is the way, which leadeth unto life, and few there be that find it.

Many times in our walk, we look at others and make a predetermined decision concerning the salvation of someone else. We do not know their walk, their circumstances, or their trials. We look and say, "That person isn't saved, or that person is going to hell." Yet are we where we are supposed to be? Self-examining questions arise—when was the last time I shared the Gospel? When was the last time I asked for forgiveness? When was the last time I prayed, and shut my mouth, just to hear from God?

For thousands of years men and women of faith have been trying to do the same thing—preach the good news of Jesus Christ and the Kingdom of God. We see this in Matthew 22:1-10. I will use a few verses, but I encourage you to read all 10, to get the full understanding. In verses *2 and 3* himself is Jesus is talking.

> The kingdom of heaven is like unto a certain king, which made a marriage for his son. And sent forth his servants to call them that were bidden (invited) to the wedding: and they would not come.

There are three important messages that Jesus is trying to help us see and understand. The first example is that of the Old Testament prophets, who continually tried to get the Israelites to hear what God wanted to do for them. God showed them miracles. God led them through the wilderness. God even wanted to speak to them, but they did not want to listen. So, God sent the next plan.

Matthew 22:4 - 5—Again, he sent forth other servants saying, tell them which are bidden [invited] Behold, I have prepared my dinner: my oxen and my fatlings are killed, and all things are ready: come unto the marriage. But they made "LIGHT OF IT" and went their ways, one to his farm [job or livelihood] and another to his merchandise [worldly possessions]:

Here we see John the Baptist and Jesus himself, trying to share with God's chosen people—the Hebrew people. They did not want to listen. God sends more servants, as we see in verse 8, 9 and 10.

Matthew 22:8—Then saith he to his servants, the wedding is ready, but they which where bidden (invited) were not worthy,

I want to stop there, notice the scripture says—were not worthy. The last servants are those today that are called to preach salvation and the good news to the Gentiles—the rest of the world.

Matthew 22: 9 - 10—Go ye therefore into the highways, and as many as ye shall find, bid (invite) to the marriage. So those servants went out into the highways and gathered together all as many as they found, both bad and good; and the wedding was furnished with guests.

In the last days, we need to understand that ALL ARE INVITED, some will come for many reasons, but not all will be saved. "Now hold it pastor! Are you saying that everyone who comes to Jesus is not going to be saved?" Let's go further. Let the Holy Spirit speak the truth to you—follow me.

Remember many come to the dinner table—banquet table, the Supper of the Lamb. Let's look and see what Jesus says?

> Verse 11, 12—And when the king came in to see the guests, he saw there a man which had not on a WEDDING GARMENT; And he saith unto him, FRIEND [Jesus calls him friend], how camest thou in hither not having a wedding garment? AND HE WAS SPEECHLESS.

We can play church, by going every week. We can read the bible, go to bible study, and even profess to be a Christian, but if we do not own the right attire, this is what will happen!

> Verse 13, 14—Then said the king to the servants, BIND [we will talk about that in a little] him hand and foot, and take him away and cast him into outer darkness; there shall be weeping and gnashing of teeth. For many are called, but FEW are chosen.

In a previous chapter, Jesus is illustrating the power of loosing and binding. The word bind is the same in that verse.

> Matthew 18:18—Verily I say unto you, Whatsoever ye shall bind on earth shall be bound in heaven: and whatsoever ye shall on earth shall be loosed in heaven.

Jesus is describing preaching the power of the gospel and the power of loosing and binding as a principal in heaven. When we share the Gospel and a person doesn't want to hear the truth, they are not only bound here on earth, but the decision they make to not accept Jesus, is bound in heaven. In contrast, the person who accepts Jesus, and walks in that truth, he is loosed (freed) here on earth and loosed in heaven also.

You may ask, what is the *Wedding Garment*? How do I get it, so not to be taken out of the *Marriage Supper of the Lamb*? We need to go back to the Old Testament scriptures to answer that question.

> Isaiah 61:10—I will greatly rejoice in the LORD, my soul shall be joyful in my God; for HE HATH CLOTHED ME with the GARMENTS of Salvation, he hath COVERED ME with the ROBE of RIGHTEOUSNESS as a bridegroom decketh himself with ornaments, and as a bride (that's us) adorneth herself with her jewels.

In the Old Testament, the Priests would adorn themselves with the *Ephod*—a garment they would put on to enter the tabernacle or the temple. You could say, the garment of salvation is the undergarment given through salvation. When you accept Jesus as your Lord and Savior, He gives you a garment of salvation. I am reminded of another garment that He gives us that we must put on.

> Isaiah 61:3—the garment of praise for the spirit of heaviness.

Think about it, you are invited to a wedding. You show up, not in a dress or a suit, but in your underwear? What do you think is going to happen? I am pretty sure, you will be asked to leave and to change. Understand, if you don't you will be ushered out of the wedding reception. Many believers think that just because you accepted Jesus, you are going to the Marriage Supper of the Lamb. Technically, you are invited, BUT there is a formal attire. Let's look at Revelations to see what that is?

> Rev. 19:7 - 8—Let us be glad and rejoice, and give honor to him; [same words as in Isaiah] for the marriage of the Lamb is come and his wife [the bride or us] hath made herself ready.
>
> Ephesians 5:26 - 27—That he might sanctify [Jesus does the work if we are willing to allow him to do it] and cleanse it with the washing of water by the word. That he might present it to himself a glorious church not having a spot or wrinkle, or any such thing; but that it [church or us] should be holy and without blemish."

What is being said here? Jesus does the work. We allow him to do the work. He removes the spots and the wrinkles, so we can come with our *Robe of Righteousness*, ready to celebrate the Marriage Supper of the Lamb. We will be coming not in our underwear, which is close to being naked?

Revelations continues.

> (verse 8) and to her was granted that she should be arrayed in fine linen, clean and white; FOR THE LINEN IS THE RIGHTEOUSNESS of the SAINTS.

Translated, submission to God, holy actions, works, and desire to be clean and holy, is the Wedding Robe.

> Revelations 16:15—Behold, I come as a thief. Blessed is he that watcheth and keepeth his garments, LEST he walk naked, and they see his shame."

In short, I pray you are understanding that it is more than just accepting Jesus in your heart. Without a doubt, that is the FIRST step.

Many never follow through after that. They say to themselves, I am going to heaven, and live a life of being a carnal Christian. They believe that just because they go to church, and try so hard to be good, they are okay. Through these scriptures, I think we can see that is not the case.

Again, in Revelation, John is sharing, in chapter three, about the church of Sardis. The scripture says,

> Revelations 3:4—Thou hast a FEW names even in Sardis which have not defiled their garments; and they shall walk with me in white, for they are worthy

The word "few" stands out. The Church, you and I, need to wake up to the truth of the whole Gospel. It is easy to hear that I just have to do this, and that, and then everything is A-OK. Being OFF THE GRID will help us zone in and learn to walk closer with the Lord Jesus. Ultimately, through this walk, we will sit down at the Marriage Supper of the Lamb, with our Robe of Righteousness on, and enjoy the time with Jesus for eternity.

The Church has accepted the world's sin, prosperity, and politically correct errors. We have embraced the world instead of being the LIGHT (in darkness) and the SALT (of the earth). Jesus said, "Salt is good."

> Luke 14:34-35—BUT if the salt have lost his savour, wherewith shall it be seasoned? It is neither fit for the land, nor yet for the dunghill; but men cast it out. He that hath ears to hear, let him hear.

Lastly,

Hebrews 12:24, 25—And Jesus the mediator of the new covenant, and to the blood of sprinkling, that speaketh. For if they escaped not who refused him that speak on the earth, much more shall not we escape, if we turn away for him that speaketh from heaven.

Jesus is calling you right now. He wants you to come to the Marriage Supper. You are invited. Please don't show up with your underwear on or you will be escorted out. Don't take that chance, be ready, be found without spot or wrinkle. Allow Jesus to do His job—clean you and prepare you. Your job is to let Him.

Chapter Seven
Conclusion

John 16:33—These things I have spoken unto you, that in me ye might have peace. In the world ye shall have tribulation; but be of good cheer, I have overcome the world.

What an assurance Jesus gives us in the last days. I have taken you through the past, the present, and the future. JESUS IS COMING, and He is coming for a BRIDE (HIS church). To be ready, we need to be OFF THE GRID. My desire is to see the Body of Christ obtain the prize—the high calling of Christ Jesus in their lives. As a pastor, and under shepherd, I see a lot of things all around me. I am not perfect, yet I strive for perfection, and to be holy, as He is holy. The Holy Spirit reveals to me many things. I pray He does to you. Each leading and each unction from Him is for a purpose. It's to GROW, to CHANGE, to BE A WITNESS, or even TO BE HIS HANDS EXTENDED. I know, whatever He does in our lives, it is for our good.

Maybe you have read this book, and you have never given your life over to Jesus. You may have gone to church, and like me, never heard, that just knowing Jesus is not enough. Through this book, I pray I have given you food for thought. Through this, you are at a place, right now, where you know you need to change. Time is short, and Jesus is calling you. Although, I grew up in a Lutheran Church, it wasn't until marriage that I became serious about understanding the Word of God. Reading the scriptures helped me understand that I couldn't save myself—I needed a savior. It was then, I truly desired more of Him. I learned that church, religion, my position as pastor, or human relationships, could not save me from eternal damnation.

I grew up knowing the Bible stories. All my years of grammar and high school, I attended church. Yet, it was one day, at an *Amway* conference, on a Sunday, I heard the words of truth. "You need to accept Jesus in your heart."

From that moment on, I understood that a relationship with Jesus was the most important. May it be today that you will want to know that peace, and joy that I have found in Him (Jesus). I would like you to read the following statements and allow the living God to speak to you, by that inner voice.

> Romans 3:23—For all have sinned and come short of the Glory of God."

The first thing—is to agree with God that you have done things wrong (that is called sin)—things like lying, stealing, gossip, etc.

The second thing—is to agree with God that I need to be born again. What is that? In John 3:1-8, Jesus is confronted by a Pharisee named of Nicodemus. Nicodemus reports to Jesus, *"Rabbi, we know that thou art a teacher come from God; for no man can do these miracles that thou doest, except God be with him."*

> And Jesus responds, "Verily, verily I say unto thee, except a man be born again, he cannot see the kingdom of God."
>
> Nicodemus asked, "How can a man go back into his mother's womb?"
>
> "Except a man be born of water and of the Spirit, he cannot enter into the Kingdom of God," answers Jesus.
>
> In John 14:6— Jesus saith unto him, I am the way, the truth, and the life; no man cometh unto the Father, but by me.
>
> John 3:16—For God so loved the world that he gave his only begotten son, that WHOSOEVER (that's you and me) believeth in Him should not perish, but have everlasting Life."

The third thing—is admit to God that you cannot do anything to have this relationship with Him. You can't buy it or earn it through works or giving.

> Ephesian 2:8—For by grace are ye saved, through faith; and not of yourselves, it is the GIFT of God.

The fourth thing—is you need to repent and ask for forgiveness.

> Luke 13:3—except ye repent, ye shall all likewise perish."

Repentance is the KEY to freedom. We hold onto things in our past and Jesus said, "When the SON *sets you free, you are free indeed."*

The fifth thing—is you need to ask Jesus into your heart and life.

> Romans 10:13 "For whosoever (that's you and me) shall call upon the name of the Lord shall be saved, (born again).

Just say to Jesus, "Come into my life. I need you. I know you died for me, rose again, and are coming back for me soon. Lord, take my life and use it for your Glory."

You are now a Child of the Living God.

> 2 Corinthians 5:17 —Therefore if any man be in Christ, he is a new creature, old things are passed away, behold all things are become new."

You now have a new life in Jesus Christ. It's simple, right?
What do you do now?

Ask God to send you to a bible teaching, Spirit-filled, church that will nurture you, encourage you, come along side you, and teach you the ways of Jesus Christ. It's called *Discipleship* or being a disciple of Jesus. Share with others that you have a new life. Beware, not everyone is going to be happy that you are now a Christ follower.

Pray, read the Bible. If you need one, contact us, and we will send you one. Importantly, trust the Lord. I have been walking with the Lord for thirty-four years (1980), and although I am a pastor and evangelist, I still have a lot to learn. So, do not be discouraged. But be encouraged, because the Word says in 1 John 4:4, "Greater is He that is within you, than he that is in the world." Start to practice speaking words of encouragement. When you are strong and ready, pray for those around you.

I want to thank you for reading and I pray that this book has changed your life, if only in a small way. I pray that this book had been an eye-opening experience. It has been a pleasure to write it. Your life will never be the same from this day forward, as you look into the mirror, and see a new creation.

Allow me to pray for you now—

"Father in the name of your Son Jesus, I come before you and thank you for the person reading this book. As you have done the miraculous in my life, I pray that you would encourage, touch, heal, and save the reader. May your blessings be upon them and your Spirit in them. I speak healing, blessings, encouragement, joy, and Life into them right now. God be with them and guide them by your Spirit. Increase their wisdom and knowledge of your dear Son – Jesus. I pray this in Jesus Name. Amen."

Please take this book and pass it on. Continue to pray for me, and my family, as we share what God has placed on our hearts. Be encouraged, one day, I hope to see you, as we walk with the One, who redeemed us—Jesus Christ our Savior and Lord.

OFF THE GRID   ERIC G. ZEIDLER

Workbook

Are you ready? Has these insights encouraged you? The following few questions are from each chapter to refresh and remind you to get **OFF THE GRID**

Chapter 1: The Way We Used to Be

John 17:15, 16—I pray not that thou shouldest take them out of the world, but that thou shouldest keep them from evil. They are not of this world, even as I am not of this world.

When we accept Jesus into our lives and become "born again" things just don't become great and everything is like a pie in the sky. Things change?

God _____ things to happen in our lives?
We need to _____ on the Holy Spirit daily.
Proverbs 22:6 "_____ up a child in the way he should go, and when he is old, he will not _____ from it"

What an assurance we have, that if, we take our family (kids, spouse) to church, over and over, they will learn valuable lessons.
Our _____ gets us in trouble.

OFF THE GRID   ERIC G. ZEIDLER

If we live after the flesh, we will _____

Jeremiah learned many valuable lessons when he went down to the potter's house. God wanted to get his attention. God used an object lesson to get him to understand.

When has God used an object lesson to get your attention? (An object lesson is when wisdom is revealed through the use of things and occurrences around us. It could be through someone's conversation. Perhaps through an object in your office or home. All of a sudden through those ordinary things, you say to yourself, "Wow, I get it now.")

Write some brief times God used these objects or saying to get you to hear Him.

_____
_____
_____
_____
_____
_____
_____

What were the series of steps that Peg taught me about Jeremiah?

You don't throw a _____ piece of clay on the wheel first.
You have to apply _____ and _____ it first.

By applying pressure and kneading it, you make the clay ready to be used. God does the same to us. When we are hard, rigid, and don't want to change, our lives seem more difficult, than if we had of allowed God to change us.

The clay is then placed in the _____ of the _____

Like the clay, when we are there, we are in God's perfect place to be used. If we are out doing our own thing, we are out of line, and that's an uncomfortable place to be.

Next comes the water, which represents the _____ of _____

When that is applied to our lives, it is easier to live a life full of Grace, Joy, Love and Peace.

After some time on the wheel, by _____ and _____ to what is on God's mind.

The clay becomes _____, and now can be _____.

Once the clay is finished being molded, it is placed into the fire. Being in the fire, is an example of us growing in God's grace and in the image of Jesus Christ. Fire refines us, changes us, and forms us into being Christ-like.

If we _____ we go back into the fire.
If we _____ we are ready to come out and be decorated and used.
When we are _____ the _____ we are in a place of humility, joy and servant hood.

Expectation can crush a dream!

Throughout our lives, there are many times, we work with, or fellowship with other people. People, in general, mean well. Consequentially, if we all are ON THE GRID, we are worldly, and fleshly minded. Describe a time when you were hurt by someone that you trusted or they broke your heart, when you did not expect it?

_____
_____
_____
_____
_____
_____
_____
_____
_____

I can get hurt when I try to please _____
God _____ you just as you are.

Our motive for work and being busy cannot be to achieve recognition from others. Being OFF THE GRID is remembering that whatever we do, we do it for the Lord. Acknowledgement from Him is greater than that of anyone.

Ephesians 2:8, 9—For by _____ are ye saved through faith, and that not of_____, it is a gift from _____. Not of _____ lest any man should boast."

Chapter 2: – Emotions

1 Corinthians 2:14 —But the natural man receiveth not the things of the Spirit of God; for they are foolishness unto him, either can he know them, because they are spiritually discerned."

Emotions are not things to play with. The enemy knows how to push buttons to make you do things that you do not want to do. God has given us emotions to help us live and enjoy this world. Contrarily, Satan uses them against us, if we allow him.

We live in two worlds, a _____ world and a _____ world. In this world (natural) we use _____ _____.

God produces in us a chemical called _____ that are designed to relieve stress. This is a problem when mixed with our emotions.

We also live in an unseen, spiritual world. Human sin also has two sources;

There is the _____ source, where Satan and principalities bring temptation.

There is the _____ source, where we make choices in response to the temptations.

Someone who mixes endorphins and emotions are called _____Christians.

Emotions change like the _____.

We cannot mix up _____ and _____.

Jesus was moved with _____

Being OFF THE GRID is not an _____ decision but a _____ decision.

Jesus was speaking to the women at the well, she was thinking in the _____ world, while Jesus was talking to her in the _____ world.

The Holy Spirit works in us the *nine Spiritual characteristics* not the *five emotional senses.* They consist of love, joy, peace, longsuffering, gentleness, goodness, faith, meekness, and temperance. We cannot buy them, earn them, barter for them, or trade for them. They are a gift to be used to operate in the Spiritual world or realm.

When we are walking in the Spiritual world, the gifts of the Spirit _____ our lives like a super saint.

The senses or emotions can play _____ on us. That is why we need to be OFF THE GRID.

CHAPTER 3: WHAT IS OF THE GRID?

1. Another word for staying OFF THE GRID, or being invisible and unnoticed is _____.

2. God told Abraham, to take his son to offer as a sacrifice. God told him to walk and ___ _____ _____ you where to go. This is being led by the Spirit of God.

3. Being OFF THE GRID is not only being obedient to God but willing to _____ _____ and _____ to His exact plan.

4. Stop thinking about what God wants. He desires our _____ _____ and _____ to get us through.

5. What are the two fundamental things needed to be OFF THE GRID.

a) _____ b) _____

6. When we are listening to the Holy Spirit, we are _____ _____ _____.

7. In Acts 16, Paul and Silas learned how to be STEALTH. What are the three things learned through the Holy Spirit.

16:6 _____
16:7 _____ _____ _____
16:10 _____

8. Paul and Silas plans were _____ and their plans were _____.

9. In the 6 Examples in this chapter, what was Jesus's one idea He tried to tell everyone. _____

CHAPTER 4: BEING THE VOICE AND NOT THE ECHO

1. When in a cavern, a mountain side, or what is it called when you say something and it returns? _____

2. The Echo is just words in space. Is there any power in the ECHO?

Yes____No____
Why?_____
_____
_____

3. In John 14:26 who is it that the Father (GOD) will send to us?
_____ _____

4. When we are ON THE GRID, are we listening to the HOY SPIRIT?

Yes____No_____
Why?_____
_____
_____

5. Another mark of being OFF THE GRID is _____ and _____ GOD'S voice.

6. When we hear a voice or echo, can it come from SATAN?

Yes____No_____
Why?_____
_____
_____

7. Can other people be the voice and the echo?

Yes____No_____
Why?_____
_____
_____

Read 2 Corinthians 11:14

8. By being OFF THE GRID, God has given each one of us the opportunity to _____ from HIM. He is asking us to be HIS _____ and not the _____.

9. In Matthew 10:16, We are told to be like a _____ and a _____

A serpent is representing _____
And a dove is representing grace by flying _____

10. Being the Voice and not the Echo is walking in _____.

11. An Echo is someone else's _____.

Read Revelations 12:11

CHAPTER 5: THE PRESENCE OF THE LORD

1. Exodus 25:8, says when we make Him a sanctuary (a place to reside), He will come and _____ among us.

2. Adam and Eve _____ with God in the Garden of Eden.

3. In order for us the Glorify God, and be in His presence we need to be _____ _____ _____, not being notice or bringing attention to us, but HIM.

4. There are 5 steps to enter into His presence:

Being _____ to get OFF THE GRID, sacrificing our time, our lives, our heart and our plans to Him.

As the brazen alter in the OT, we need to self-examine ourselves like standing in the mirror, and _____.

Then there is the showbread, or the Bread of Life, which represents _____. So, the third step is _____ with Jesus.

What is the lamp unto your feet? _____, and it guides us in the right direction. So, we need to read and understand it.

Before the veil in the temple, there was an alter of incense. This represents our _____ time. The quiet, intimate time with just Jesus and you. This is being OFF THE GRID.

5. Luke 9:25 sums up the topic of this chapter. Summarizing the KEY to being OFF THE GRID, is getting rid of _____, being the _____ and not the echo, and getting rid of or dying to _____

References

All biblical scriptures are from the King James Version of the bible unless otherwise noted

JOURNEY NOTES

Write your journey here as you draw closer to the Lord by spending time off **OFF THE GRID**

_____
_____
_____
_____
_____
_____
_____
_____
_____
_____
_____
_____
_____
_____
_____
_____
_____
_____
_____
_____
_____
_____
_____
_____
_____
_____
_____
_____
_____

ABOUT THE AUTHOR

Eric G. Zeidler is an ordained minister and has been in full time ministry preaching the Gospel for 24 years, locally in the Delaware Valley area and around the world in Haiti, Romania, Bahamas, and the East Coast of America. He currently pastors The River Church in Penns Grove, NJ which he started 20 years ago.

He accepted Jesus Christ as his savior and Lord in 1980 at an Amway Conference in DC, and has never looked back. Eric has started many ministries over the years dealing from food distribution, to homeless outreach, to joining with other ministries to work together as the Body of Christ. CTF-TV a 24/7 radio/internet program is another way he shares the message of the Gospel around the world, while helping others who have God given talents.

Eric's passion is "the Body of Christ" working with other churches, ministries, and organizations to be the light to a hurting world.

Pastor Eric, his ministry, or The River Church can be contacted via the below information:

Pastor Eric Zeidler
PO Box 486 Swedesboro NJ 08085
www.ctf-tv.com
(Facebook) River Church
www.therivernj.com

The River Church Salem
91 Walnut Street
Salem, NJ 08079
(856) 275-7279

The River Church
222 South Broad St.
Penns Grove, NJ 08069
(856) 514-2206

FOR OTHER BOOKS BY THIS AUTHOR VISIT
<ins>WWW.CTF-TV.COM</ins>,
FACEBOOK.COM/OTGBOOK,
CTF_TV@YAHOO.COM, AMAZON,
VOICECNC.COM

This book was published by:
The Glory Cloud publications LLC
P.O. Box 193
Sicklerville, NJ 08081
www.theglorycloudpublications.com
vof1@aol.com

For additional information about us and how to obtain other literature, or how to publish your life story, testimony, miracle report, biography, fiction, or children's story book, please write or email us at the above addresses.

*Psalms 68:11
*Habakkuk 2:3, 4 *2 Corinthians 1-7
*Jude 22

With our Voice and His Glory, by Faith
Making a Difference in the World

www.ingramcontent.com/pod-product-compliance
Lightning Source LLC
Chambersburg PA
CBHW050603300426
44112CB00013B/2050